MY SPORT
MOTOR RACING

Tim Wood

Photographs: Chris Fairclough

Franklin Watts
London • New York • Sydney • Toronto

© 1989 Franklin Watts

Franklin Watts
12a Golden Square
London W1R 4BA

Phototypeset by Lineage, Watford
Printed in Italy by G. Canale & C. S.p.A. - Turin
Design: K and Co

ISBN: 0-531-10828-7
Library of Congress No: 89-50201

Illustrations: Simon Roulstone

The publishers, author and photographer would
like to thank Andy King, Dennis Rushen, Gavin
Jones, the mechanics of the Concept 3 Racing
Team and Cathy Jaggs in the Press Office at
Silverstone Racing Circuit for their help and
co-operation in the production of this book.

The racing driver featured in this book is Andy King. Andy was always interested in motor racing. He began by racing karts at the age of 15. After five successful years he moved up to Formula Ford. He did well in the Junior Championship and then finished second in the Esso Formula Ford Championship in the following year. He moved up to Formula 3 in 1986. He started the season well by winning three races, but his car began to suffer from mechanical problems. He raced for the British Telecom team for a season. Recently Andy has been looking for a major sponsor to back his career. He combines this with working for car manufacturers, demonstrating new road cars and teaching new drivers at the Silverstone Racing School in England.

3

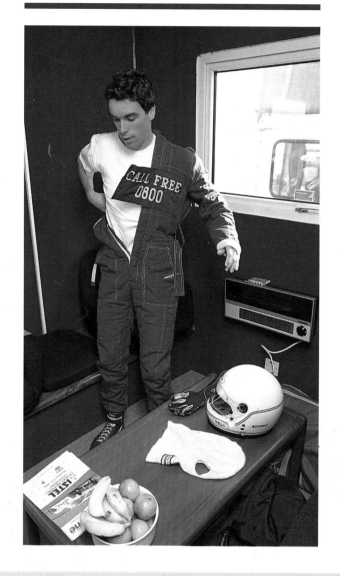

I am a racing driver. Tomorrow I will drive
in a Formula 3 race. Today is a practice day.
I get ready by putting on my fireproof
overalls in the team truck.

In the pit garage, the mechanics are giving the car its final check. One has just put the advertising logos on the side. He gives the body a last polish.

I adjust my fireproof driving shoes. They are very light and comfortable. I am resting my foot on one of the tires. Racing tires are made of a special sticky compound that helps them grip the track and improves cornering.

I have to remove the steering wheel to get
into the car because the cockpit is so small.
The seat and pedals have been specially
adjusted to suit me.

I put on my fireproof balaclava. Like many racing drivers, I am quite superstitious. I always put on my equipment in the same order, as I believe this will bring me luck.

I put on my helmet and gloves. I am ready for my practice run which will last for twenty-five laps. During my drive, I will find out how well the car is going. I will return to the pits if any last-minute adjustments are needed.

More about motor racing

Motor racing is a very expensive sport. Each driver drives for a racing team. The most experienced and successful drivers are paid by the racing team to drive for them. But "up-and-coming" drivers have to pay the racing team to be allowed to drive their cars.

A racing team provides a team truck, racing cars, mechanics and all the spare parts. During a Formula 3 season of eighteen races, the driver might pay his or her racing team about $320,000 to drive a car. In order to raise this large sum, the drivers look for sponsors who will pay their expenses. In return for this money, the driver carries the sponsor's advertising on his or her car and clothing.

Driver's eye view

This is a view of the cockpit of a Formula 3 racing car.

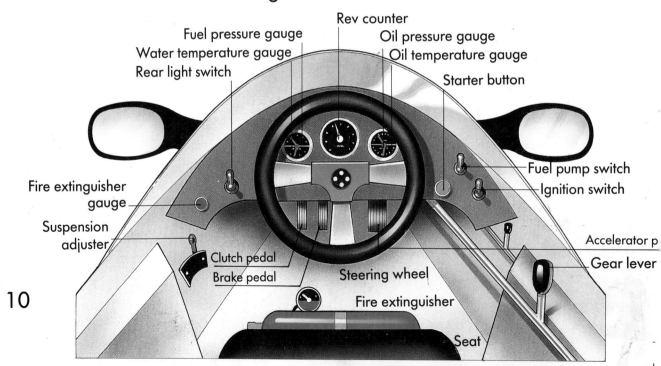

Rev counter

Fuel pressure gauge

Oil pressure gauge

Water temperature gauge

Oil temperature gauge

Rear light switch

Starter button

Fire extinguisher gauge

Fuel pump switch

Ignition switch

Suspension adjuster

Accelerator p

Clutch pedal

Gear lever

Brake pedal

Steering wheel

Fire extinguisher

Seat

The Silverstone Racing Circuit.
The circuit hosts both motor
racing and motorcycle racing
competitions.

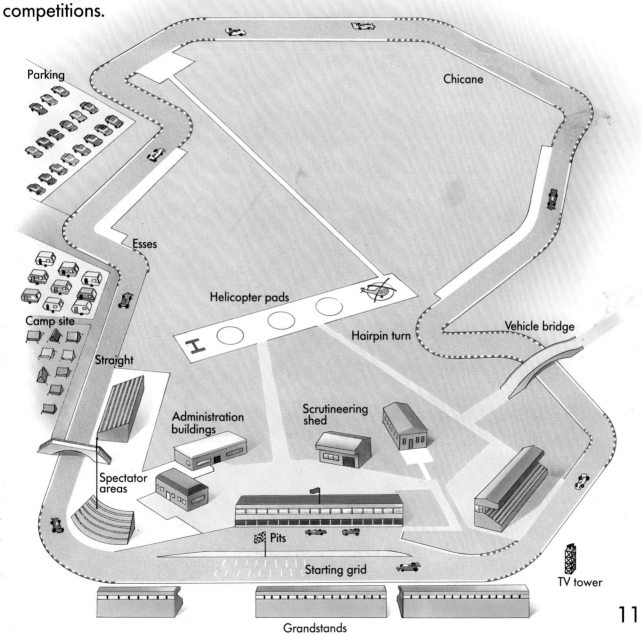

Parking

Chicane

Esses

Helicopter pads

Camp site

Vehicle bridge

Hairpin turn

Straight

Administration
buildings

Scrutineering
shed

Spectator
areas

Pits

Starting grid

TV tower

Grandstands

The cars all wait in the pit lane for the signal to go on to the circuit and begin the practice run. The noise is deafening as the drivers rev their engines.

Once the signal is given, the drivers begin their practice laps. A computer times each car. The drivers with the fastest times will start tomorrow's race at the front of the grid.

My chief mechanic checks my lap times with a stopwatch. He holds out a lap board with my lap time on it. This tells me that I drove the last lap in 1 minute and 33 seconds, an average speed of 186 km (116 miles) an hour.

Unfortunately, during the practice I skid on a corner and crash. A tow truck brings the car back to the pit garage.

The team truck is full of spare parts and tools. The mechanics will have to work very hard to repair my car in time for tomorrow's race. I must try to get a good night's sleep.

After inspecting the car carefully, my chief mechanic begins to remove all the damaged parts. He is confident that he can repair the car before the race.

By early the next morning, some of the work
has been done but there are still many
repairs to finish. The car is raised so that
18 the mechanics can work on it more easily.

The carbon-fiber nose section was not damaged in the crash. The aluminum wings are taken apart and hammered back into shape.

The damaged suspension units are replaced
with new ones.

A special tool is used to measure the angle of the rear wing. If the angle is wrong, the car will not corner properly and will skid at high speed.

By the time I arrive at the circuit, the car is ready. I get in and my chief mechanic helps me fasten my seat belts and replace the steering wheel.

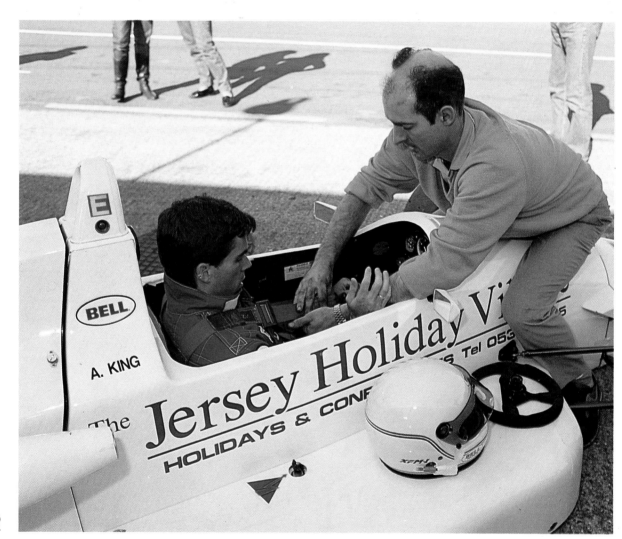

Before I drive to the starting grid, the team manager gives me some advice. He talks to me through a microphone that is connected to my helmet. He can hear my replies through his earphones.

At the starting grid, track marshalls guide each driver to his place. For this race I start on the twelfth row.

When the cars are in position, engines are switched off. My mechanics rush out to make last-minute adjustments. One lets some air out of the tires to help them grip the road better.

The cars do a warm-up lap. This allows the
drivers to check that everything is working
properly. At last, the cars take their
positions on the grid. The drivers rev their
26 engines, eager to be off.

The red lights turn to green. The race has started. The cars roar off down the straight, past the grandstand, towards the first bend.

With only three laps to go, I am in fourth place. Driving around this bend, I realize that there is something badly wrong with the brakes of my car. I must make a pit stop.

The mechanics soon realize that major repairs
are needed. The race will be over before the
car is fixed. I have no choice but to retire
from the race. I hope I will have better luck
next time.

FACTS ABOUT MOTOR RACING

The first motor race was probably held in the United States in 1878. The race was from Green Bay to Madison, Wisconsin, a distance of 323km (201 miles). The winner was a steam powered car.

The first race held on a closed circuit was an 8km (5 mile) race held in Rhode Island in 1896.

The fastest ever lap speed reached was 403.8kph (251mph) by Dr. Hans Liebold of Germany who was driving a turbo-charged Mercedes-Benz around a high-speed track at Nardo, Italy.

The fastest overall speed for a Grand Prix race on a modern circuit is 235.4kph (146.3mph) achieved by Nigel Mansell driving a Williams in the Austrian Grand Prix in 1987.

Racing cars compete in different classes according to their engine size, engine power, body size, tire size and shape. Here are some of the cars you may see at a race meet:

Formula 1 – 3500cc highly-tuned engine, specially built for Grand Prix motor racing.
Formula 3000 – 3000cc tuned engine specially built for motor racing.
Formula 3 – 2000cc tuned engine based on various makes of production car such as the Volkswagen Golf GTI.
Formula Vauxhall/Lotus – 2000cc slightly-tuned engine based on the Vauxhall Astra.
Formula Ford 2000 – 2000cc slightly-tuned Ford production engine.
Formula Ford 1600 – 1600cc slightly-tuned Ford production engine.

GLOSSARY

Accelerator
Pedal that feeds more fuel to the engine and so increases the speed of the car.

Cockpit
The driving compartment of a racing car.

Formula 3
A group or class of racing cars which are all powered by similar 2000cc engines.

Grid
Rows of starting places on a racing circuit. The drivers with the fastest practice lap times start the race at the front of the grid.

Lap
Once around the circuit.

Mechanic
Someone specially trained to repair cars, motorcycles or other machines.

Pits
The area of a motor-racing circuit which is reserved as the place for racing teams to garage and repair their cars.

Team truck
A large truck and trailer used for transporting a team's racing cars, carrying spares and providing a rest area for the drivers and mechanics.

Wings
Flat fins that are attached to a racing car — two small ones at the front and one large one at the back. When the car moves, the air passing over the wings presses the car more firmly onto the road, improving road-holding and cornering.

Index